This Journal Belongs to

Published by

Real Joy Publications

Made in the USA
Coppell, TX
01 June 2020

26820478R00067